ThinkBanking
Corporate & Webbing

50 Secrets to
Success in the Digital Age

ThinkBanking

&

Corporate Webbing

50 Secrets to

Success in the Digital Age

A. M. Young, Ph.D.

M. D. Hinesly, M.B.A., D.B.A.

M. J. O'Brien, M.Ed.

Young, Amy M

Hinesly, Mary D

O'Brien, Michael J

ThinkBanking & Corporate Webbing
50 Secrets to Success in the Digital Age

ISBN 0-9981878-0-1

STAR PG

www.starpg.com

For our families...

Contents

Preface

Human memory has a clear evolutionary advantage. It has allowed us to store our past experiences, learn from them, and improve our performance in the future. It's the survival of the fittest.

Once upon a time, when our lives were simple, human memory was enough for us to learn from our experiences in the world. Yet our world has outgrown our memory capabilities. Evolutionary change takes far too long to keep pace with the changes of the past half century. The complexity of our world has grown exponentially, and we are continually bombarded with information, of which we are able to retain and use an infinitesimal amount.

Corporations face a similar problem. As they have grown over the past half century, companies have become international behemoths with regional branches dispersed throughout the world.

Competitive forces have expanded beyond national borders. Running a company requires considerable coordination among dispersed divisions and partnering companies.

Given the size and scope of companies, it is impossible to fully compile the vast amounts of corporate information. Failure to connect the dots results in missed market opportunities, operational inefficiencies, and wasted resources.

But both individuals and corporations have learned how to use technology to make up for the slow change of evolutionary adaptation. We now have personal devices that serve as repositories for our social interactions, financial exchanges, entertainment, and real-time monitoring of personal health data. Every day – if not every hour – we use digital memory to augment our biological memory systems.

Companies have similar digital memory systems, referred to as Big Data. These digital memory systems help companies store and learn from information to improve future performance.

Big Data allows companies to compile and analyze previously disconnected information about their sales, production, and customer preferences and habits.

We see improved business performance in terms of companies' ability to quickly respond to new market conditions, anticipate customers' needs, and create new products and business models.

Companies using Big Data to improve future performance are the ones that will survive in the Age of Information. It's survival of the fittest.

Yet despite the benefits of Big Data, these digital memory systems do not capture companies' most valuable information. Far more valuable than sales records and online customer tracking is the knowledge that resides within the minds of employees.

Critical data walks out the door every day, and no firewall can stop that. Sometimes the holders of such critical data, feeling disengaged and disenfranchised from the behemoth corporation, even walk out your door and in through the door of your competition, never to return.

What if there was a way to capture the most valuable information a company has and put it to use? This book introduces you to two new uses of digital technology: Corporate Thinkbanking and Corporate Webbing. These enable companies to compile, integrate, and apply employees' knowledge and goodwill to solve the most pressing corporate problems.

Successfully using this technology requires more than just data science, however; it requires an understanding of the human element.

New World Order in the Age of Information

1. It is all about speed and agility.

What are the new rules of business for the digital era? Which companies will survive and which will go by the wayside? Will my company survive?

These big questions gnaw on the minds of business leaders. It is common knowledge that the digital revolution has happened, and information age is here; yet few fully understand what this means for business. We can see that digital technology is continuing to change how businesses are run. We sense the change underfoot – the reshuffling of what creates competitive advantage and what is falling away. But few know what it takes for a business to survive in the digital era.

This book is about the secrets to business survival in the 21st century: what you need to know about digital technology to survive as a business leader.

Business survival has always involved speed and flexibility – the ability to see new opportunities and respond faster than competitors. Digital technology has made the game of business far more complex, because it provides far more information than we have ever had before. In fact, the most perplexing challenge facing companies right now is disconnection from their own purposes, due to growing complexity. We now have so much information that it is hard to connect the dots to make out the bigger picture.

Moreover, the greater size and complexity of corporations has led to employees also feeling disconnected from company goals, although the term "disengaged" is more commonly used to describe this condition.

Innovative Fortune 500 companies have learned from tech start-up companies how to use digital technology to connect these disconnections. As a result, they are able to respond with speed and flexibility. They can make the meaningful connections among the many points of information to see market opportunities, new innovations, and ways of improving efficiencies.

They have also learned to use digital technology to build employees' emotional connection to the company, thereby leveraging employee knowledge and goodwill to achieve common goals. Connecting the disconnected is how to win the game of business in the information age.

The book has been written so you can quickly read a handful of take-away points when you have a few minutes. Feel free to skip around.

2. Companies can no longer dominate a market merely with a superior product.

Or at least not for long.

Previously, long term competitive advantage could be based primarily on having a superior product. Just build a better mouse trap, and the world will beat a path to your door. Bringing a great product to market at just the right time made it possible to dominate a market for a good 15-20 years. This product-based strategy meant that a company could survive by focusing heavily on research and development while neglecting other aspects of the organization, such as service. Service could be subpar without jeopardizing a company, as long as the company had a product that provided strong and long-lasting market dominance.

That world is gone. It is still essential to have a great product; however, having a great product provides you only a ticket to the show. The window of opportunity to capitalize on a product has shrunk considerably – in some cases, it's as short as six months. Companies are constantly struggling to distinguish their product from competitors and any differentiating value is likely to be short-lived. Once the window of opportunity passes, products function more like commodities because there is a marginal value difference between a company's product and its competitors'.

3. The true value of a company lies within its intangible assets.

For the past 30 years, the size of market capitalization backed by physical assets has fallen dramatically to around 20%. This means that the true value of a company is far more likely today to be based on intangible resources. In the past, intangible assets consisted primarily of intellectual property, customer relationships, and technology.

Today, however, some of the most important resources consist of the managerial and organizational factors that enable employees to work together with speed and agility. These "people centered" strengths include new leadership and management approaches, energizing work cultures, and employees' knowledge and workplace engagement. Such assets were previously viewed as "extras" not relevant to profit. In today's world, an agile and engaged workforce is essential for surviving in the rapidly changing marketplace.

In addition to being more relevant, these intangible assets are being used by companies in more creative and complex ways than ever before. Brand, for example, has always been an important company asset, but now companies are using it to do far more than just increase sales. Today savvy companies, such as Starbucks and Nike, are using their brand to expand into marketplaces outside their core business.

This ability to adapt and expand into new markets requires more than just brand and resources. Organizations need to have a well-integrated and coordinated system of intangible assets that leverages talent, digital technology, and employee engagement to perform at a higher level and under unexpected circumstances.

4. Aligning and realigning to new market opportunities is what wins the day.

For a company to be successful in the 21st century, it needs to be able to:

- quickly identify and respond to potential market opportunities
- innovate internally rather than just acquire
- scale successful innovations through standardization, coordination and enhanced communication across organizational silos
- repeat this process of rapid adaptation on an ongoing basis

This is not the first time that companies have needed to "up their game" in response to a changing world. Following the industrial revolution, companies grew from small "mom and pop" stores or small organizations. These new corporations had operations that were too large to coordinate without a more controlled and organized approach. In response, new business models emerged in the early 20th century that emphasized hierarchical structures, command and control leadership, and an impersonalized workforce carrying out routinized tasks.

The result was an increase in organization and coordination across the company and subsequently an increase in operational efficiency and cost savings.

Companies are being tested again with the need to find a better approach to organizational coordination. This time the test is much more daunting and paradoxical. Companies need to develop a systematic, repeatable approach to organizational change by creating the structure, processes, and organizational norms that foster quick adaptation.

Similar to the challenge companies faced in the early 20th century, success depends on the system being understood and adapted throughout the company to ensure alignment and coherence.

5. New tools and new ways of working together create agility.

Creating speed, flexibility, and organizational alignment requires both the digital technology and a new approach to employee engagement.

All too often companies focus solely on the technology, as it is more tangible and easier to change. But the second half of the equation – how employees work together and align to the company – is far too often overlooked.

The result is that many digital networking initiatives fail before ever being given a chance.

The new digital technology allows for a better way for employees to communicate and collaborate with each other using networking communication systems. The technology provides a means of connecting employees' knowledge that is currently dispersed throughout the organization.

Yet the technology is not sufficient for connection to occur. Employees need to be proactively willing to share their knowledge.

Currently employees' lack of engagement with the technology is the number one challenge facing companies looking to achieve digital collaboration.

Companies that are succeeding in this space have learned to address both the technology and employee challenges by adapting a new way of working together.

6. Social media IS for employees.

Many companies are wary of letting employees use social media, but social media – or at least a special type of social media designed specifically for companies – is the ideal communication channel for employees.

Digital Enterprise Systems are social networking systems designed to be used for communication within companies. These platforms provide a secure means of sharing information, and companies retain ownership of all information. (In contrast, Facebook and other public networking sites retain ownership of information even when the sites are used for business purposes.)

You do not hear the term interconnectivity every day, yet you likely reap its benefits throughout your day.

Social media platforms such as Facebook, Twitter, or LinkedIn – all of which are based on interconnectivity – enable us to communicate with our entire social network with just a couple of key strokes.

Such interconnectivity through the World Wide Web provides us with immediate access to an overwhelming amount of information. If we want to rally a political group or let the world know about the poor service we received at a restaurant, we have access to our very own soap box.

Interconnectivity, defined as the state of being digitally connected to a network, has permeated our lives so drastically and quickly that it is easy to forget what life was like without it.

Interconnectivity has also profoundly changed the rules of business by creating new approaches to competitive advantage, business models, and leadership and management practices.

Whole industries have been disrupted; just think what has happened to the music industry, bookstores, newsprint, advertising, and traditional taxi transportation. What you have witnessed with these industries is just the tip of the iceberg.

Within organizations, companies are using interconnectivity to improve how employees work together to achieve a common goal. These internal applications of interconnectivity can be just as valuable as the external ones, because they enable large companies to respond with speed and agility.

7. Interconnectivity fundamentally changes how we communicate.

Before the Internet, anyone wishing to communicate with a large group needed access to a mass communication channel, such as radio, television, or a printing press. The average citizen had few or no options to share information with the masses.

Today the average citizen can distribute text, images, or video within seconds to anyone in the world with Internet access. Depending on the person's reach, or whether it goes viral, the average citizen has a means of speaking to the world.

Interconnectivity also gives rise to collective wisdom, a whole new powerful source of insight. Collective wisdom, a concept popularized by Surowiecki in his book The Wisdom of Crowds, holds that the aggregation of information from groups leads to better decisions than what could be made with any single individual.

This is because groups of people, located in multiple positions, have access to more information than any individual.

Interconnectivity enables a company to access far more information than what was available from single channel mass communication systems. It has become common practice for companies to use interconnectivity to gather more information from and about their customers.

Just as valuable, though, is its use for collaboration within the organization. When employees "pool together" what they know, the company is able to make faster, better decisions than before.

The company is thus able to quickly re-align with changing market conditions, because employees are "on the same page."

Consider the purpose of organizations: to achieve a common goal that is too large for any one individual.

Interconnectivity is ideally suited for use inside a company because it provides a way for any one employee to share valuable information with the rest of the company within seconds. It is now possible to function as a single unit; an ability that serves as the basis for organizational agility.

8. Tech start-ups developed a more efficient way of running organizations.

Most technology companies that emerged after the internet became popular were created with networked communication in mind. Consider Google, one of the most agile companies in the world, which has successfully leveraged interconnectivity to create competitive advantage, whether it be through Big Data, new business models, or digital organizational agility. Initially, Google was just Sergey Brin and Larry Page in a Stanford dorm room.[i] Soon Susan Wojcicki and others joined, but the company was still quite small, and no formalized approach was needed for the group to work together. Sergey and Larry's management approach was simple: hire bright and creative talent, give them freedom, and communicate openly to ensure they are heading the right direction. Project management was simple, too: current projects were listed on a spreadsheet and made available for everyone to see and debate in terms of importance. Sergey and Larry's approach was based on what seemed to be working for their small team and their intuitive business acumen. They did not have formal business degrees, which in hindsight was likely an advantage.

As Google continued to grow, Jonathan Rosenberg, who had a solid business background, was brought in to provide structure to Google's approach. However, when he presented his strategy to Sergey and Larry, they rejected it. With an MBA from University of Chicago, Jonathan brought to the table a plan based on the traditional model of structured departments, a multi-layered management structure, and decisions made by a small executive group at the top. Sergey and Larry sensed that this traditional approach would not work with their highly creative and brilliant group of computer engineers, which they knew was the company's most valuable asset. They pushed back with the understanding that a better approach could be created. In this sense, not having a business background or a preconceived idea of what management "should look like" opened them up to explore alternative possibilities. Google went on to intuitively create a new approach to organizing how employees worked together. As with many other tech startups emerging in the 2000s, interconnectivity was at the heart of this new management approach and how their employees worked together.

We can see the impact interconnectivity has had on society in terms of social movements and politics (e.g., Black Lives Matter). What is less apparent is the impact it is having on how companies operate internally. We can see the results of this change in the competitive advantage these newer companies have over ones built on traditional management models. Tech startups leveraged interconnectivity to create a more efficient way of organizing how employees work together. This approach was present at the birth of Google and companies like it. As these companies have grown, this new management model has become firmly entrenched in their organizations.

9. Many innovative Fortune 500 companies have adapted the tech start-up approach.

Eventually Google and other tech startups grew big enough to pose a threat to older more traditional companies. Many "traditionalists" dismissed these tech startups early on because their founders were young and didn't look or act like traditional CEOs, and their workplaces looked like adult playgrounds with unusual employee perks and causal office attire. Eventually, though, the success of the tech startups was hard to overlook. The new products, business models, and management practices built on interconnectivity provided a clear advantage.

Recognizing this, many well-established companies tried to replicate their approach. Some, only seeing the "Google difference" at a superficial level, changed their workplace environments by adding the unusual office perks.

Not surprisingly, these superficial changes had no impact on workforce collaboration, engagement, and productivity. However, other companies accurately identified the fundamental difference in their management and organizational approaches.

Today, some of these Fortune 500 companies have been able to take this fundamental difference to the next step by actually recreating the approach within their organization. This is a significant feat that should not be overlooked; being born digital is far easier than transforming to digital.

Transforming means that the company must continue to operate at the same production level using the old system while gradually integrating the new system.

Leadership must have a clear vision of the transformation and convince the organization of its merits during the growing pains of the trying transitional period while the seeds for success are being planted. The upside is that the companies that successfully make the transformation become nimble giants, able to disrupt whole industries.

They have the capital and brand that comes with being a well-established international company and the speed and dexterity characteristic of a small startup. The combination is formidable.

Creating Business Value by Connecting the Disconnected

10. Networked communication is a game changer.

Exactly how are companies creating business value from interconnectivity? The secret lies in the fact that interconnectivity and a network communication system are better at distribution within large groups.

Information sharing in traditional organizations is based on a model similar to the wheel. The inner position is the CEO, who communicates to the C-Suite, who then passes along the information to the respective corporate divisions. Information from the "frontline" of the organization is passed up through the chain of command. Information rarely flows across divisions with this arrangement.

Types of Communication Networks

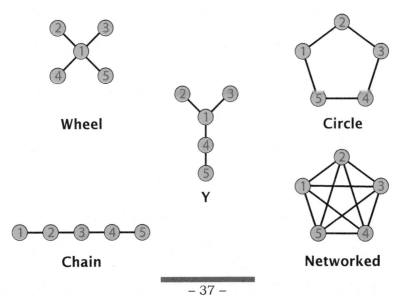

Wheel

Y

Chain

Circle

Networked

As companies have grown over the past century, the challenge of information distribution within the organization has also grown. Today with the mega-corporations, disconnection between management and labor and between co-workers is all too common. It is easiest to evaluate such disconnection in terms of information distribution:

- How often are employees delayed because they do not have the information they need?
- How often are they delayed because they didn't have the information in a timely manner?
- How often has work been replicated in different parts of thc company because employees didn't know what was happening in other divisions?
- How often have employees worked on a task only to find out a week later that leadership has changed directions and the work is no longer needed?

The significance of disconnection within a corporation is enormous when you begin to consider how widespread lack of timely information has on employees' performance.

Now consider the financial impact of disconnected employees. The percentage of employees who know their company's mission statement is at a dismal low of 41%.

If employees are unaware of the company's mission statement and vision for the future, how can they possibly ensure that their work contributes to the common goal of the company?

Employees' disconnect from the company affects the bottom line, because they are focusing their time and effort on what they assume is the common goal, which may or may not hit the mark.

11. Big Data creates value by linking disconnected information.

Although we most often we think of Big Data in terms of companies collecting external information, such as customers' online shopping habits, Big Data can also be used to compile information coming from within the company. It involves compiling digitized information from various divisions throughout a company, such as sales, customer service, manufacturing, and shipping.

Value is created by "connecting the dots" and having a more comprehensive, up-to-date picture that improves the quality and speed at which employees complete their work.

The potential for Big Data to create value for a company is substantial. Having real-time information means that employees can make decisions faster, resulting in decreased down time in supply chains and decreased time to market for new product launches.

Knowing about changing market conditions in real time means that employees can recognize and seize market opportunities quickly. Likewise, redundant efforts across silos are less likely when employees are better informed about what is happening in other divisions of the company.

12. Corporate Thinkbanking creates value by linking employees' recorded knowledge.

Just as corporations are gaining value through Big Data, they can create value by digitally linking employees' knowledge of the company. Company knowledge includes employees' insights and what they have learned about technical matters and how the company operates.

Company information, on the other hand, is the data that a company collects as part of the ongoing operations, such as financial records, sales records, etc.

Whereas Big Data involves compiling and distributing company information that has already been digitized, Corporate Thinkbanking does the same with employees' knowledge that also has been digitized, such as electronic documents of operational procedures, reports, etc.

Often referred to as knowledge management, this method of creating organizational agility is not as well-known as Big Data, but is quickly spreading.

Creating a Corporate Thinkbank entails building a digital repository that retains employees' knowledge in a way that facilitates quick and easy retrieval by coworkers. Business value is created when knowledge is shared and applied across silos.

Cross-pollination of ideas not only increases the possibility of organically grown innovation, but it also eliminates wasted effort and resources as a result of duplicated efforts.

13. Corporate Webbing creates value by linking employees' undocumented and overlooked knowledge.

If Corporate Thinkbanking compiles employees' knowledge that has been documented, what about the often-overlooked knowledge that employees possess that has never been recorded? Although this knowledge is intangible, we consider it to be far more valuable to a company.

An employee's undocumented knowledge consists of the knowledge that has accumulated over the course of employment at a company. It might be highly specialized, technical knowledge or tactical knowledge about day-to-day operations. It can also include knowledge of the company's clients and their particular preferences. It may be implicit

knowledge of "how to get things done" in a company, such as who the real leaders are (who often are not the ones with the titles) or who has connections with employees from another division who could help solve a problem.

This begs the question:

Could your company find a way to better capture and use this information?

The reason why this company gem has been overlooked for so long is that there has, until recently, never been an easy way to capture it. It would require managers to know the information that employees need to complete their jobs better and faster. Then, knowing what the information needs are, the manager would have to ask all other employees if they have a solution. The manager's time would be consumed with serving as an information router system.

Remember, without network technology, a manager does not have access to a mass communication channel. Of course there is email, but think about how full your email box is already. Email doesn't really work well as a mass communication channel due to information overload.

The solution to this problem is Corporate Webbing. Networked communication enables employees to use the corporate social networking site to tap into the minds of fellow employees. That is, the need for an information router is eliminated. Instead, employees – who have a better idea of what information they need – can make direct requests to other employees, who already know what they know. Network systems avoid information overload by including better ways to categorize, catalogue and retrieve information.

14. Corporate Webbing creates value by linking employees' goodwill.

The second underutilized resource of a company that is just as valuable – if not more so – is the goodwill of employees. If capturing company knowledge involves reaching employees' minds, capturing goodwill involves reaching employees' hearts.

Concepts such as employee engagement, motivation and commitment are measures of the extent to which employees bring their hearts to the workplace. Employee goodwill is activated when they go "above and beyond" the prescribed job requirements to assist colleagues and customers. It is also present when employees take personal responsibility to ensure that the company provides superior services or products. Indeed, employee goodwill is often the defining element that differentiates exceptional companies from those that are good or average.

Corporate Webbing allows for the sharing of employees' goodwill, which has the potential to start a contagion of positive energy and boost employee engagement and performance. Often referred to as "online social collaboration" or "digital collaboration," these initiatives use social networking platforms to foster employee communication and collaboration.

Currently most companies attempting Corporate Webbing fail to ever achieve the desired results.

		What Is Shared	How It Works	Business Value
Management Driven ↑	**BIG DATA**	Digitized information	A digital infrastructure that collects & distributes information automatically	Innovation, insights, real-time customer service, reduced time to market
	CORPORATE THINKBANKING	Employees' knowledge that has been digitized	An online repository for employees' knowledge that already exists in a digitized form (e.g., documents)	Innovation, reduced silos & redundancy, greater distribution of knowledge
	CORPORATE WEBBING - KNOWLEDGE	Employees' knowledge within their minds	A digital networking system that enables employees to share information currently stored in their minds	Innovation, reduced silos & redundancy, greater distribution of knowledge
↓ *Employee Driven*	**CORPORATE WEBBING - GOODWILL**	Employees' goodwill	A digital network system that enables employees to share goodwill, assistance, or inspiration to others	Improved employee engagement and subsequent performance; building energy contagion

In fact, we have found that even companies manufacturing and selling the technology have been unable to create thriving online social collaboration communities, which reinforces the notion that this is not an IT challenge but a people challenge.

Corporate Webbing can be far more challenging to master than Big Data and Corporate Thinkbanking, as the value is driven almost exclusively by employees. Companies that have been able to successfully implement Corporate Webbing have identified the motivators and barriers to employees proactively sharing their knowledge and goodwill on company networking systems.

(We share these with you in sections 43-45, below.)

Reasons Why Most Companies Fail

15. They begin by asking about the technology.

At some point it will be necessary to consider technology, but it is a mistake to begin with this question.

It's similar to when people adapted to using word processing software instead of typewriters. It was a big leap to go from a typewriter to using a word processer on a computer. You had to learn a new approach that was fundamentally different.

If you were still at the point of trying to figure out how to use the Wite-Out on your screen to make a correction, you could not appreciate the merits of the latest version of Microsoft Word. You had to start with the basics. It seems so easy now, but people had to learn a different way to prepare documents.

Instead of putting a sheet of paper into the typewriter before typing, you had to adjust to watching the text appear on a screen as you hit the keys on the keyboard. The keyboard itself was different, with the keys often closer together and requiring much less force from your fingers. The concept of "saving" a document was new. (Why would you save a document? Where is it going anyway?). It was mindboggling that you could retrieve what you wrote previously, make a few changes, and send it to a printer. It was a fundamentally different method of writing.

For many people, the change in how you prepared documents changed how you wrote. Before this innovation, you felt a strong incentive to be satisfied with the first or second draft. You wrote the first draft with pencil and paper.

Changing paragraphs, or even moving sentences around, required scribbling in the margin or physically cutting up the paper to move ideas around. You couldn't get a clear sense of the final document until it was retyped. After that, any other weaknesses in the structure or word choice didn't seem worth changing, because you would have the retype the whole thing again.

After the switch to word-processors, you could formulate ideas as you wrote. You could move words or sentences around to try may different scenarios. Ultimately, this improved the quality and speed of employees' writing, which thereby increased the efficiency of the entire company.

The point is – the first thing you needed to know when you transitioned to word processing from a typewriter was that it was a fundamentally different approach, not what was new in Microsoft 5.5 from the previous version.

The shift to networked communication is similar, yet it will be more dramatic and comprehensive. With word processing, the change was in how individual employees got work done. With networked communication, the change is in how employees work together to achieve a common goal. The change is more complex and far-reaching, as it involves groups rather than just individuals. Accordingly, the rewards are even greater.

Your first objective is to understand how communication and collaboration are fundamentally different with network communication. You also have to understand how the organizational context – leadership, management, and organizational culture – impact network communication, because we are now dealing with group processes. The next step is to think about how the new approach creates efficiencies and potential business value within your organization.

Then you are ready for a discussion about technology.

16. They look to what competitors are doing.

Business leaders also make the mistake of looking to what their competitors are doing without ever taking a good look inside the company. Again, this is a mistake.

Knowing what others in your industry are doing can provide ideas, but these solutions may not be the best for your company. The reason is that cookie-cutter solutions don't work with digital technology. The technology must be tailored to the company, not vice versa.

The best way to use the technology depends on your corporate vision, strategic plan, strengths, resources, and pain points. You want to use the tools to either achieve your corporate strategy or to solve a pressing pain point. These usages will be unique to your company.

If a competitor's approach won't help your company achieve an important goal or solve a pressing problem, adopting it will only create extra work for your employees. (When you do use the technology to address a pain point , make sure that your employees perceive it as a solution; otherwise, they will perceive it as wasting their time.)

17. They think digital agility is only about technology.

Using digital technology to be agile and nimble is often more about the people than the technology. However, it depends on where the information is coming from and whether it currently exists in a digital form.

Big Data Projects are primarily technological and management challenges. The information already exists in a digital form within the corporation rather than within the minds of employees. These projects involve a reconfiguration of how corporate information is collected, compiled, and distributed.

The bulk of the work falls on IT leaders and likely a consultant in digital architecture who need to identify new ways of consolidating and distributing information. The challenge involves understanding the company's current technology, anticipating future technology trends, and finding the most cost-effective redesign. Management must also oversee the redesign of the procedures employees will use to collect and use the information. Leadership needs to determine why the project exists in the first place: How can the company create a strategic advantage by having a more complete picture? The demands on employees, in learning new procedures, are relatively minor.

In contrast, with Corporate Thinkbanking and Corporate Webbing, value is created only through active participation by employees.

		What Is Shared	Primary Organizational Challenge
Technology and Management Driven	**BIG DATA**	Digitized information	**Technological** – Designing a digital chassis that capitalizes on the corporation's unique strengths
	CORPORATE THINKBANKING	Employees' knowledge that has been digitized	**Managerial** – Redesigning how depts. and regions share, distribute, and access information
	CORPORATE WEBBING - KNOWLEDGE	Employees' knowledge within their minds	**Leadership** – Creating an organizational culture that minimizes departmental and regional competitiveness and fosters employees' proactive engagement
Employee Driven	**CORPORATE WEBBING - GOODWILL**	Employees' goodwill	**Leadership** – Creating an organizational culture that minimizes departmental and regional competitiveness and fosters employees' proactive engagement

These projects involve more of the human element, because they require understanding what fosters or stymies employee engagement. Time and again, companies fail to recognize the importance of the human element.

Corporate Webbing, in which employees share goodwill with coworkers, requires the highest level of employee engagement. These initiatives require companies to have exceptionally high levels of employee engagement. As leadership is the primary driver of employee engagement, Corporate Webbing is thus primarily a leadership challenge. Leadership must provide employees with a reason to care – to go above and beyond the call of duty – if Corporate Webbing is to thrive.

18. They focus on the tool, rather than what is done with the tool.

Thinking that digital agility involves only the introduction of new technology, companies fail to realize the importance of the other half of the process: changing how employees work together to achieve common goals.

Digital technology is just a tool, much like a hammer, pencil, or lever. We don't expect great things to emerge from these tools, of themselves. Instead, great things can emerge when people figure out new ways of using a hammer, pencil, or level to achieve a purpose.

Value is created when a company finds a new way to leverage digital technology to achieve a goal that has a high impact on the company. Network technology requires a new way of organizing employees toward a goal, one in which employees learn new ways of interacting with colleagues. The assembly line was a game changing invention, but it would be worthless if workers had not also learned a new way of working together.

19. They assume that the company's most valuable information is in their data systems.

It is easy to focus on what is tangible, such as the information that a company collects as part of daily transactions or website visits. But what if a company's most valuable asset is not readily apparent?

Big Data has received the most attention for revolutionizing business, yet knowledge that employees have accumulated over the course of their employment is generally far more valuable. In addition to being overlooked due to its intangibility, managers often underestimate its extent, given the impossibility of comprehending the full extent of what an employee knows, especially a very long-term employee.

Yet, one measure of the tacit knowledge of employees is the cost associated with employee turnover. When an employee leaves a company, the new employee experiences a learning curve as they "get up to speed." Getting up to speed is just another way of describing the process of acquiring the undocumented knowledge that the previous employee had learned.

By conservative estimates, the cost of employee turnover is one-fifth of an employee's salary.[i] When considering the cost of replacing an entire workforce as a measure of their collective worth to a company, it becomes clear just how valuable undocumented knowledge is.

Imagine how much company knowledge is held within the mind of one employee who has been employed at the firm for 10 years. What if you could capture just 10% of that knowledge and distribute it to other employees to apply to their work? What if you could reap the rewards of 10% of an employee's knowledge with 10% of your employees?

Capturing even a small fraction of the knowledge within an organization can serve as a very powerful force toward improving the efficiency of a company. Yet, most organizations are currently running with ineffective, leaky information systems that result in poor employee coordination, wasted time and effort, and missed market opportunities.

20. They assume employees will easily adopt new technology.

Employee adoption is one of the most cited reasons for a digital network initiative to fail.[iii] It may be referred to as "employee non-compliance" or a company's "cultural issues," but employees' reluctance to adopt the new technology is the most likely culprit for low return on investment.

Employees resist adapting to new technology for a variety of reasons. Some of them are straightforward, such as the learning curve associated with using the new technology. Other reasons are covered in sections 43-45. Training sessions and persistence are often adequate to address this problem.

Big Data, which simply requires employees to adapt to a new system and procedures, is far more likely to be successful than other initiatives. Corporate Thinkbanking and Corporate Webbing make fundamentally different demands on employees than Big Data in expecting them to become more proactive in asking for and giving knowledge and assistance to colleagues and to change in their relationship to the company.

Not surprisingly, these initiatives are therefore much more likely to fail. In fact, 90% of digital collaboration initiatives fail when adoption issues are not considered[iv].

It is far more complicated to "retrieve" knowledge from employees than it is to retrieve information from data files. Employees are not machines; they have needs, motives, and fears that can make it more difficult to "extract" knowledge. Oddly, it is just as challenging to get employees to request information they need[v]. Later in this book we explore further why employees are so "temperamental" and reluctant to cooperate with the new communication systems.

Success is dependent on understanding the conditions that foster employees voluntarily asking for and sharing knowledge online. Key to success is understanding human nature and the impact of workplace dynamics.

21. They do not budget and plan for organizational adaption.

It is not surprising that companies fail to budget and plan for the organizational and employee adoption of the new approaches. Without understanding upfront that agility is just as much of a human challenge as a technological development, minimal (if any) resources are devoted to changing the organizational norms, beliefs, and climate.

To do this, without giving the digital networking initiatives a real chance to succeed, and then claim that the technology has been overrated, is like planting a tree, never watering it, and then concluding that trees never grow.

Bottom line: companies need to budget as much or more resources to organizational and employee adoption as they do for the technology.

Data Science: Getting the Technology Right

22. Target important business challenges.

The first question companies should ask:

How can a better distribution of information, knowledge, or goodwill be used to achieve an important corporate goal for the next five to ten years?

This is a leadership question. To ensure that digital technology achieves a ROI, it has to be applied to a problem that has a significant impact on the company's standing.

Take for example the following business objective: A company has decided that they want to distinguish themselves from competitors with superior customer service. They want to become #1 in customer service within the next five years.

Here is what they should be asking:

- How are we currently falling short on customer service? Poor response time? Poor rates of follow-up? Having customers deal with five different employees before getting an answer?
- How could we better distribute the information we have to achieve this?
- How can we better coordinate the work among employees who interact with customers to achieve this?

The answers to these questions provide direction on how to best leverage the technology for business value.

23. Identify the untapped resources.

By this point, you should have a better idea of what you need, because you will know why you are using the technology. You also need to know what untapped resources are available.

One resource that is commonly overlooked is social capital, resources that flow through networks of relationships[vi]. Social capital includes knowledge, ideas, advice, opportunities, contacts, and emotional support. These resources exist throughout every organization, yet they are rarely considered or purposefully applied to corporate challenges.

Not all social capital in an organization is easy to find. Identifying available information is relatively easy, by conducting an audit of information collected by different divisions of the organization. Mid-level management should be able to supply this information.

Identifying available knowledge is more challenging. Even if employees' knowledge has been documented, this documentation may not be on the radar of managers.

Even more challenging is identifying implicit employee knowledge. Only employees can provide this information. Likewise, identifying employee goodwill can be daunting.

If your company is designed to allow employees to flourish, employees will volunteer to share with you the knowledge and assistance they can provide the company and coworkers. Sections 33-50 go into greater detail about how to design your organization to support this natural human proclivity to share, help and cooperate.

You may not be able to fully identify the social capital within your company at this point. A fuller understanding of the depth of resources available is only possible after employees choose to share them.

24. Determine the type and level of change required.

Once you have identified how to best leverage the technology to create value for your company, and you have taken a preliminary assessment of information and knowledge that is available, you are better able to understand the needed change.

The type of change needed is highly dependent on whether it is a Big Data, Corporate Thinkbanking, or Corporate Webbing project. With Big Data projects, management must also identify a new approach to collecting and using information from the data system. If IT has a strong centralized corporate presence, consistency throughout the organization will be more likely, which means that much of the infrastructure will be in place. If IT has a more localized presence, considerable digital architecture will be required, and the chance of incompatibility between systems across divisions or regions will be more likely.

With Corporate Thinkbanking and Webbing, management will need to create new procedures and processes for employees as they enter or retrieve information from the system and play a role in monitoring activity on the repository (i.e., the bird's eye view). Depending on the current state of the organizational climate, high levels of change may be necessary at the leadership level.

		What Is Shared	Primary Organizational Change Required
Technology and Management Driven	**BIG DATA**	Digitized information	Reconfiguration of how digital information flows and is integrated and distributed across functional areas
	CORPORATE THINKBANKING	Employees' knowledge that has been digitized	Establishment of new procedures and policies regarding the uploading & retrieving of documents
	CORPORATE WEBBING - KNOWLEDGE	Employees' knowledge within their minds	Creation of a highly collaborative culture that encourages employees to proactively share what they know with colleagues
Employee Driven	**CORPORATE WEBBING - GOODWILL**	Employees' goodwill	Creation of a highly collaborative culture that encourages employees to proactively assist colleagues and clients by going "above and beyond" prescribed job requirements

If employees have an unfavorable opinion of leadership and the organization in general, leadership will need to take significant steps to change the culture, policies, and behaviors giving rise to these beliefs.

If employees currently have a reactive approach to their work, significant training and demonstration of the authenticity of the new standards will be needed, to spur the employee initiative that drives Corporate Thinkbanking and Webbing..

25. Work with CIO when making decisions about technology.

Most modern CIOs want to partner with others in the C-suite, yet they continue to suffer from the perception of being a service unit. It is true that the IT must continue to maintain the technology systems that allow the day-to-day operations to continue. Yet this is not all that the IT department has to offer.

IT departments now deserve a seat at the table where strategy decisions are being made, because technology has become a central player in creating strategic advantage. Only when business leaders work in conjunction with their CIOs are new innovations created that leverage a company's strengths to seize market opportunities.

26. Understand what communication technology your employees actually use.

Do you know what communication technology your employees actually use? Just because the technology is available to them, do not assume that employees are actually using it. The only way to really know what they are using is to conduct a communication audit.

A communication audit studies the flow of information within an organization by focusing on the nitty-gritty of how work gets done. Employees are interviewed to identify what tasks they are responsible for, what information they need to complete these tasks, and where they get this information.

With the information collected through the audit, you can assess whether the current system provides the most efficient and effective method of achieving key organizational goals. We have yet to conduct a communication audit that didn't reveal a difference between managements' perception of how work is accomplished and what actually happens.

Getting
the Human
Element Right

27. Balance right management, leadership and culture

Understanding the human element means getting three elements right: management, leadership, and culture. When these three elements are working well, employees thrive. When employees thrive, they go above and beyond job requirements and share their minds and hearts.

Once this hidden lode is mined, the technology provides the means of distributing these employee-generated resources throughout the organization. The following tips are geared toward getting management, leadership and culture right.

What Management Must Do

28. Focus management on the who, what, and when of getting things done.

The focus of management should be on the concrete: specific actions that can be easily measured and tracked. Management sets the foundation for Corporate Thinkbanking and Corporate Webbing by establishing:

- how these repositories will be created (planning and organizing)
- who needs to do what to create, contribute, and use the repositories (staffing and directing)
- when these tasks will be completed (controlling and monitoring)

Management sets up the systems, monitors, and, when mistakes and negative deviations occur, directs employees to get performance back on track. Because management activities are more concrete, management tends to receive more than its fair share of organizational attention and priorities.

When creating Corporate Thinkbanking and Corporate Webbing, companies need to lead the transition of managerial systems and processes, rather than give obsessive attention to the usual managerial systems.

29. Apply managerial practices with intention for maximum agility.

Along with the efficiencies of cost that come with mega-corporations are many inefficiencies due to poor coordination, redundant efforts, and wasted time. Inefficient managerial practices sometimes continue simply because they are an ingrained part of the organizational culture. Because business survival today is largely dependent on quick organizational adaptation to a rapidly changing market, companies need greater flexibility to respond to market demands. And yet, just as importantly, large corporations need to maintain the stability, efficiencies, and optimization that come from strong managerial oversight.

Key to maintaining equilibrium is the ability to manage the constant tension between the needs for agility and stability. Instead of applying managerial practices out of habit, the level of oversight – whether it be through project oversight, strict adherence to policies and practices, or resource allocations – needs to fit the needs of the situation. Company leaders need to be mindful of why a particular management approach is being used to ensure that the degree of oversight is most appropriate to the need for agility or stability.

30. Achieve organizational alignment for real-time operations.

Companies need to learn how to execute operations in real time. It started with real-time advertising and is now moving to other business functions.

Real-time advertising began in 2013 with Nabisco's Oreo Super Bowl Blackout Twitter[vii] Commercial. In case you missed it, imagine this: You're watching the Super Bowl and their lights go out. You turn to Twitter to get the latest and find "You can still dunk in the dark" with a picture of an Oreo cookie and a glass of milk. How brilliant is that? It's called real-time advertisement.

Nabisco pioneered it, but Coca-Cola made it an established marketing approach in 2014 with their FIFA World Cup commercials[viii]. During the World Cup, Coke commercials brought you clips of viewers from around the world as they watched the same games. You felt a collective spirit humming around the world, all brought to you by Coke.

What is even more remarkable is what happens behind the scenes to allow real-time advertising to happen. How are companies able to condense what used to take months to produce into hours? Successfully executing real-time advertising requires reconfiguring the legal, social media, marketing, and advertising departments into teams with representatives from each function.

They work together in command centers with large screens projecting social media feeds from around the world.

We have entered the age of real-time operations. After being heralded within marketing, by 2015 it started becoming the approach for all aspects of a company, at least for the digital dynamos.

Take for example how Sprint responded in real time following their launch of the "All In" plan featuring David Beckham in commercials. Early bloggers disliked the fact that the plan had a video streaming limit of 600 Kilobytes per second. Within a day of its launch, Sprint responded to criticisms by eliminating this barrier.

How does a company with 36,000+ employees change its course within a day? A quick decision is easy to make, but did they actually have the technology to lift the streaming limit? Would the plan still be profitable? Could they get the word out to all employees of this change?

For large companies to operate in real time, they need communication technology throughout, yet they also need all employees working together. Digital agility means having the technology and the organizational alignment required to move in unison.

31. Fail fast, fail often...but respect the limits of your industry.

Favorite advice given to companies working on agility is, "Don't be afraid to fail! As long as you are learning and adapting, you are going forward!"

Many are still hesitant to follow this advice because the penalties can be severe. Some industries have a zero tolerance for mistakes. We appreciate that pharmaceuticals, chemical companies, and hospitals are less tolerant of employee mistakes, as lives are at stake. The challenge is finding the right balance between trying new approaches and needed caution. Each industry will have a unique equilibrium between purposeful risk taking and a cautious "wait and see" approach.

However, other reasons for not using the "fail fast, fail often" approach are not justified. For example, a workplace culture in which employees are afraid that their reputations and careers will be jeopardized can lead to a stymied company that falls behind its competitors. This is a problem with the culture of the company, rather than a legitimate need for cautiousness.

What Leadership Must Do

32. Focus not just on getting there first, but on how you become first.

When companies speak of leading in digital agility, it means they want to be a trailblazer on the cutting-edge of leveraging technology for business agility. They are not thinking about how the head of the company will relate to the employees of the company. But this is exactly how companies become trailblazers: the head of the company must be able to create an organization in which employees can thrive.

Currently most employees are not highly engaged with their company's mission or leaders. Companies have not provided them with adequate reason through the kind of demonstrated commitment to a cooperative culture that supports full employee engagement.

Exceptionally high level of employee engagement provides the energy need for Corporate Thinkbanking and Corporate Webbing to thrive.

Most companies focus on the management needed for Corporate Thinkbanking and Webbing, because management is far more concrete and tangible than leadership. Doing this without achieving high employee engagement is like buying a high-end luxury car but forgetting to fill the gas tank.

33. Keep the structure, change the mindset.

Leading in digital agility does not necessarily require a change in the structure of the organization; instead it requires a change in the mindset, a different approach to thinking about how value is created.

The traditional hierarchical company often uses a "command and control" leadership model. The leader at the head of the company commands employees to complete tasks, and managers control employees so they comply. The company thrives when leaders and managers are able to do their jobs well, and employees outside of these positions bring a relatively low level of value to the company.

Perceived value is shaped in a pyramid, with those closer to the pinnacle of the pyramid being more valuable to the company. The bottom of the pyramid provides the foundation that enables to the top to thrive.

Digital agility requires companies to adopt a new leadership model in which value is created throughout an organization by connecting the dots, and all employees are therefore positioned to bring value to the organization.

In an organization functioning as a collective, employees at the frontline – customer service representatives, technicians, floor operators – play a very important role. For example, it was a waiter at a TGIF restaurant that noticed that a new entrée wasn't selling well because customers didn't like the taste of …. Getting this information to corporate headquarters was instrumental to changing the recipe quickly.

34. Nourish your organizational tree.

Instead of thinking of the value of the company in the shape of a pyramid, use the analogy of a tree. In this model, leadership serves as the tree trunk. By setting the mission, values, and strategic direction for the company, it creates the foundational bedrock of the company to guide and structure it as a whole.

Management serves as the branches that grow from this foundation as they execute the direction established by leadership. Employees are the leaves of the tree, where the action is. Much of the photosynthesis that provides life to the tree happens in the leaves. When a company is thriving, you can see it in the health of the leaves. With a solid tree trunk and strong branches, the leaves of the tree grow and flourish.

Yet the success of a tree depends much more on what is not visible to the eye: the root structure. A tree is only as strong as its root structure. The leaves of the tree are not able to get the nutrients needed to thrive without this healthy root structure.

The root structure represents the culture of an organization: the unspoken beliefs, values, and norms that shape how employees act within the company every day.

In the modern era, the tree analogy provides a much better mental picture of a thriving organization than the command and control model.

35. Lead.

Recognizing that the most valuable resource is employees does not mean that the need is any less of a need for leadership. Leaders need to set a clear vision for how the company is to move forward.

Companies are unable to thrive without a central figure to identify and articulate a clear vision. Other skills are just as important: providing a reason for why employees should care about the vision and empowering them to execute it.

Although claims that the hierarchical structure needs to be eliminated for flatter organizations have become more frequent in recent years, the hierarchical structure is not inherently stifling in the current business landscape.

Instead, it is the misperception that value is only created through the top echelon of the hierarchy that prevents companies from thriving. Leaders should seek the counsel of others, but the final decision about the vision must come from the leader. Collaboration happens in the execution of the vision.

36. Create a positively deviant organization.

Positively deviant organizations don't just focus on solving problems. Instead, as Kim Cameron has illustrated, they continue to strive to become extraordinary companies that bring out the extraordinary from their employees[ix].

A company investing in the technology for Corporate Thinkbanking and Corporate Webbing also needs to invest in creating a positively deviant organization to be able succeed in these initiatives.

Most companies have a "good enough" approach: As long as we have eliminated problems, we have done our job. Recognizing that employee absenteeism has made it difficult to complete projects on time, they focus on preventing illness among employees. Problem solved.

Positively deviant organizations go a step further: They ask how can we enable our employees to thrive? How can we create an entire workforce that is fully engaged in their jobs? The first approach gets warm bodies into the building; the second approach means that the place is humming with activity.

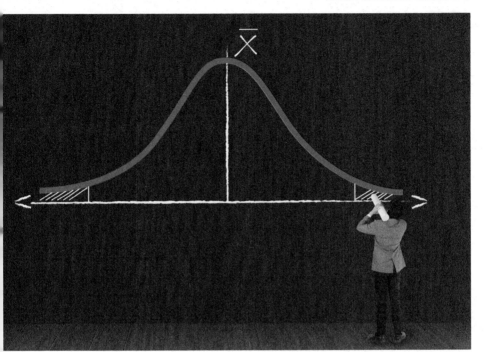

37. Give employees a reason to go the extra mile.

As we've mentioned, Corporate Thinkbanking and Webbing require employees to proactively and voluntarily share their knowledge and goodwill. Bob Quinn, an eminent scholar in the field of leadership and organizational transformation, notes,

> *"Just as people have discretionary money that they can choose to spend in the economy, they have '**discretionary energy**' that they can choose to bring to work."*[x]

This discretionary energy is the life blood of the networked organization, the necessary ingredient for agility in the marketplace. Employees may be willing to dig down and go the extra mile for a company, but they need a compelling reason to do so. This means providing an environment in which employees are more than just engaged; they are thriving and feel passionate about their work.

When companies are in the normal zone, employees do not bring their discretionary energy to work. The problem in this case does not lie with the employees.

At thriving organizations, employees want to bring this extra energy to work because leadership has given them a compelling reason to do go "above and beyond" their job descriptions.

38. Earn your following.

Leaders need to have a strategic vision that moves the company forward. Not only do they need to consider the business environment outside the company, they must attend to the internal needs of the company. They must be skilled at communicating their vision throughout the organization so that everyone is working towards the same goal. It not just a matter of employees knowing where the company is going, however; a leader also needs to communicate to employees why it matters and why they should care.

This begins by being a leader who is worthy of being followed. Remember, to get employees to give you their expendable energy, they have to want to go the extra mile for you, the company, and their coworkers. You have to earn that.

The way to earn a following is as old as humankind:

- Great leaders must be authentic. This means being straightforward and honest. Employees know when you are not. They tolerate leaders who are not straightforward – it is either that or quit. But leaders who are not authentic will never gain the trust of employees.
- Great leaders must be humble. They need to recognize that they play an important role in the company, but that value is created through all the employees.
- Great leaders must be motivated by the good of the company, not just their own self-interests. Employees can tell the difference. Why should they use their discretionary energy for the good of the company when the leaders' true mission is to promote their own careers?

39. Unify around the company's higher purpose.

Employees bring their expendable energy to work when they feel connected to the company's higher purpose, values, or vision. It is easier for employees to feel a connection to nonprofit companies. Employees work for organizations promoting literacy because they feel passionate about enabling others to read. Employees work for organizations promoting clean water because they feel passionate about environmental causes.

For other companies, employees may have a difficult time connecting to the company's higher purpose, if they even know the company's purpose. Company profit is not a good enough motivator for employees to connect.

However, employees can connect to for-profit companies in many ways, as long as there is more to the mission statement and company values than simply being profitable. Google's mission statement "to organize the world's information and make it universally accessible and useful" enables employees to feel that they are helping others by providing access to information.

Even financial companies can have mission statements that provide employees with a higher purpose. "To bring clients superior returns" enables employees to connect to a higher goal.

What really matters, though, is whether the mission statement and corporate values are living beliefs in a company or just words written on a page.

40. Help employees connect their job to the higher purpose.

How many employees in your company understand how their day-to-day activities contribute to the company's purpose? If your company is like most companies, the answer is very few.

When employees can't see how their day-to-day tasks connect with the higher purpose, they do not see a reason to bring their discretionary energy to work. They may bring the extra energy for a personal purpose; for example, an office administrator may find it personally fulfilling to create order and consistency within the department.

Employees may also bring their expendable energy to assist a coworker. A shift worker might be willing to stay longer if a coworker has a sick child and needs to stay home. In such a case, however, the worker is going the extra mile for the coworker, not for the company.

Imagine having a company where employees are so committed to the company that they all chip in for the good of organization. This isn't just a fantasy; this is what it means to have a positively deviant organization.

41. Appreciate employees to increase their engagement at no extra cost.

Let employees know that you appreciate the efforts they make. It seems too easy to be true, but it matters.

When you take the time to acknowledge employee efforts, it enables them to feel part of the larger picture and connected to the company's purpose.

Remember, one of the downfalls of today's large global corporation is that employees have become disconnected.

Aside from financial compensation, employment can provide other benefits, including two of the most important human needs:

- A connection to a social group.
- A connection to a higher purpose.

Acknowledging employees' contributions strengthens both connections without costing the company a cent.

Create a Positive Culture

42. Foster high quality connections.

How strong are the relationships among employees at your company? If they are superficial with little emotional investment, the social capital at the company is inadequate for Corporate Thinkbanking and Corporate Webbing to thrive. Getting online sharing to occur first requires time spent offline forming high quality connections.

High quality connections (HQC) is a term used to describe powerful connections between people that have a strong and lasting positive impact on both. HQC within the work environment are a fundamental source of social capital that facilitates the sharing of information, ideas, advice, support, and connections. Although these relationships remain professional, they are powerful in enhancing employee engagement and coordination among teams, as well as strengthening employee commitment to the organization.[xiii]

HQC often exist within a company, regardless of whether they are fostered by a company, but the benefits derived from these HQC will build loyalty between those employees rather than furthering organizational goals. The company benefits from HQC when leaders choose to promote these types of relationships within the company so that they become an embedded component of the organizational culture.

43. Recognize and reward helping behavior offline.

When assessing company needs, an important first step is to examine how employees work together offline. If there is little helping behavior offline, we know not to expect it online. Our work begins by understanding the organizational culture that inhibits employees willingness to help others.

Generalized reciprocity occurs when a person does something of value for another without an expectation of an immediate return.[xiv]

Such generalized reciprocity has the power to produce extraordinary results by increasing the volume, velocity and efficiency of exchange of social capital throughout networks. Wayne Baker, an eminent scholar in this area, has created a tool, the Reciprocity Ring™, which organizations can use to facilitate generalized reciprocity.[xv] The tool has been used widely, and the online version is currently in beta testing.

You only need to see a group of employees put the Reciprocity Ring into action to witness the power of the generalized reciprocity. All participants are asked to submit a request. It can be professional or personal, relatively straightforward or outlandish. All other participants are instructed to consider how they or someone in their network could help make this request a reality.

Surprisingly, at least 80% of participants get a valuable lead. But the real power of generalized reciprocity is evident when the outlandish requests – such as seeing a Bangle Tooth Tiger in the wild – are fulfilled. Humans are hardwired for reciprocity because we are social by nature. When the obstacles to sharing are removed, our natural inclination to assist others flows naturally.

To foster generalized reciprocity, you need to make it the company norm to offer help. Is sharing behavior valued? If employee receive no acknowledgement or appreciation when they help colleagues, the implicit message they receive is that helping colleagues is not behavior that will lead to a promotion.

44. Make it the norm to ask for help.

Skeptics of the Reciprocity Ring find it hard to believe that people would go out of their way to help. They are correct that getting the process of generalized reciprocity going in a group is challenging. Yet it is not because participants are unwilling to help; it is because participants are reluctant to ask.

Curtis Conley, who has worked for Fortune 500 companies to facilitate online sharing among employees, has had similar experiences with getting employees to ask for help from colleagues using online digital communication tools.

> *"When employees have a question or a request, they will commonly contact me, hoping that I will post it. It is hard to get employees to ask because it makes them vulnerable. The fact that they did not have the answer becomes common knowledge. Employees don't know whether it will be used against them at some point."* [XVI]

Corporate Thinkbanking and Corporate Webbing cannot thrive in companies where it is important to maintain appearances. Employees will only ask when they can trust that it will not jeopardize their reputation or standing in the company.

45. Don't let knowledge be used for political power and advancement.

Is knowledge a scarce commodity in your organization? Is it hoarded and used to wield political power and career advancement? If so, don't expect employees to share knowledge.

Leaders can inadvertently create organizations that incentivize employees to withhold information from others.

The company may be overwhelmed with data, but employees will hoard valuable "insider" knowledge for when they need it. A highly competitive culture is created in which it is impossible for an organization to function as a singular entity. Who has time to focus on industry competition when there is so much infighting?

The solution is to distribute as much information as possible so that it no longer can be used for infighting. Of course there are limits to what can be shared – for example, some financial documents may be too sensitive to distribute widely. However, make it a default to share information so a reason is needed to not distribute widely.

46. Foster a culture of growth.

Whether leaders realize it or not, the culture established within an organization indirectly shapes employees' performance and work engagement. When an organization creates the belief that individual effort makes a difference, motivation among employees increases, and the result is a more productive workforce. Conversely, when an organization creates the belief that individual effort does not make any difference, employees' motivation and performance decreases.

Organizational culture impacts how employees engage within a company in five key areas:

Efficacy: does the organization encourage employees to approach tasks with a sense of confidence and resilience?

Goals: does the organization encourage members to move toward goals by being focused, proactive, and innovative?

Approach: does the organization encourage employees to balance task accomplishment and the need to engage others with integrity and transparency?

Relationships: does the organization encourage employees to work well with others through teamwork, mentoring, and sense of regard for all employees, regardless of position?

Altruism: does the organization enable employees to find a higher purpose and connect meaning to the work they do?

Employees may come to a company with personal beliefs that either liberate or limit their performance. But the shared beliefs within a company create a powerful force that can affect how employees approach their work and colleagues. These beliefs are established by leadership, but are commonly "driven home" by the day-to-day interactions employees have with their managers.

Most companies remain in the dark about employees' perceptions of their work environment. Taking the time to learn whether the company liberates or limits employees' beliefs is the necessary first step.

The Cultural BluePrint™

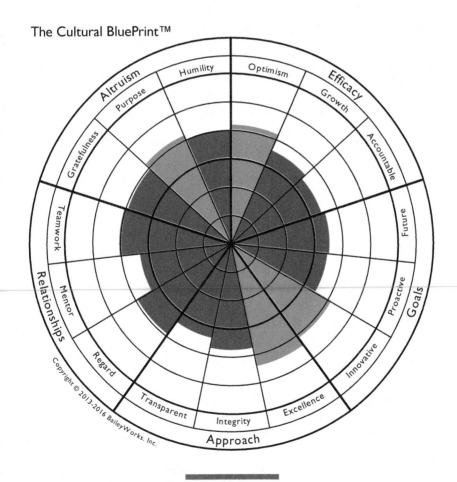

Change Management

47. Start with pain points and pilot projects.

New ideas for big projects with big budgets and wide-sweeping change are hard to sell. You end up fighting an uphill battle. Instead look for the easy wins.

There are two ways to create easy wins:

- First, start with the pain points, the areas in the organization quickly identified as thorns in the sides of key decision makers regarding the proposed investment in digital technology. Removing a thorn – even a small one – will get their attention.
- Second, start with small projects and refer to them as pilot projects. Decision makers are far more likely to try something new if they don't have to commit to a significant long-term financial investment.

Whatever project you choose, you must be able to deliver. Your objective is demonstrate what can be done while asking for only a small commitment on their part.

48. Identify early adopters.

Not all employees react to new technology the same way. Some, called innovators, are quick to jump on board. These are the people who get the new gadgets before everyone even knows that it exists. Early adopters, who enjoy being trendy, like getting the technology just as it is taking off. Those in the early majority are comfortable with progress yet need to see solid benefits to the new technology.

The late majority are conservative pragmatists, whereas the laggards hold out to the bitter end. Laggards were just accepting the concept of a cellular phone while everyone else had Smart phones.

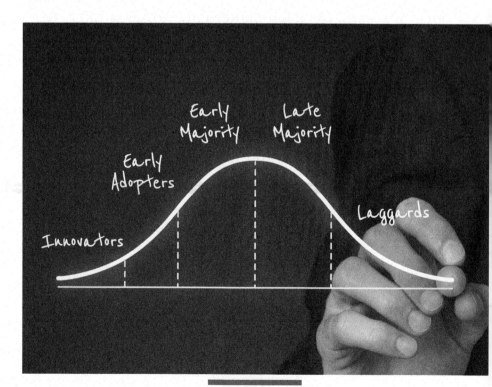

The concept that not all individuals adapt to technology with the same ease was proposed by Everett Rogers in 1962. His initial ideas were not informed by adoption of the cell phone, of course, but by the adoption of farm equipment in the Midwest United States.[XVII]

Do you know which employees are your innovators and early adopters? Are you targeting your effort on getting these employees onboard with the new technology, or are you targeting all employees?

Focus your efforts on the first three categories. Innovators will immediately be onboard because they like trying new gadgets. Early adopters will be onboard as soon as it becomes trendy. Early majority will be onboard as soon as there is some demonstration of the benefits. By that point, you will have reached a critical mass.

Malcolm Gladwell refers to this as the tipping point,[xviii] the point at which there is enough momentum for change to be self-perpetuating.

49. Identify the real influencers in your organization.

We all know some people who are more influential than others in the company. This has nothing to do with formal roles and everything to do with how connected they are within the company.

Some employees are well connected with others and stay fully in the loop with what is really happening at a company (which may not be the official story). Other individuals stay at the periphery, choosing to focus on their job and know only a few people in the company, mostly those within their department or team.

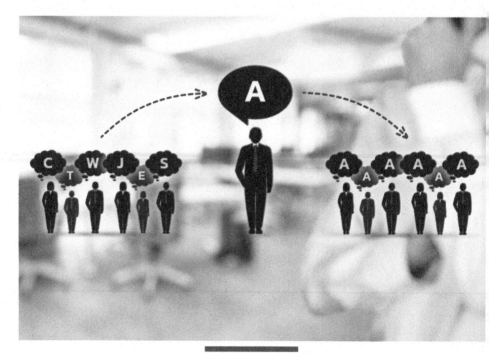

Network analysis provides a method to identify which employees have high social influence, given their strong connections throughout the company. If you want to manage change effectively, you need to identify those with strong network connections that span across the organization.

Similar to technology adoption types, you can use this information to focus on those employees best able to bring about contagion. When adoption reaches the tipping point, the momentum will help enable the change to have a life of its own.

50. Ask employees for help.

When leadership is faced with a crisis and what appears to be insurmountable odds, have they considered asking the employees for help?

Knowing the power of generalized reciprocity and networks, it is not farfetched for an employee to have the answer. Likewise, it is not farfetched for employees to come together to work in collaboration to make the seemingly impossible happen.

The obstacles to unleashing the power of the collective spirit within a company are imaginary. Leaders often assume that they will be perceived as weak if they ask for assistance. The truth is that leaders will be humbled, but employees will be empowered.

When leadership has established a direction, empowered their employees, and provided them with the tools for real-time coordination, insurmountable odds can be overcome.

Endnotes

i   Eric Schmidt & Jonathan Rosenberg's (2014) How Google Works and Laszlo Bock's (2015) Work Rules! Insights from Inside Google that Will Transform How You Live and Lead.

ii   Boushey, H, Glynn, S.J. (2012). There are Significant Business Costs to Replacing Employees. Center for American Progress. http: https://www.americanprogress.org/wp-content/uploads/2012/11/ CostofTurnover.pdf

iii   Ragab, M.A.F & Arisha, A. (2013). Knowledge management and measurement: A critical review. Journal of Knowledge Management Review, 17, 6, 873-901.

iv   Bradley, A. & McDonald, M. (2013). The Social Organization: How to Use Social Media to Tap the Collective Genius of Your Customers and Employees. Cambridge, MA: Harvard Business Press.

v   Baker, W (2000) Achieving Success Through Social Capital: Tapping Hidden Resources in Your Personal and Business Network. Hoboken, NJ: Jossey-Bass.

vi   Adler, P.S. & Kwon, S (2002). Achieve success through social capital: Prospects for a new concept. Academy of Management Review, 27, 17-40.

vii   http://www.wired.com/2013/02/oreo-twitter-super-bowl/

viii   http://www.coca-colacompany.com/coca-cola-unbottled/coca-cola-brazils-real-time-marketing-wins-gold-effie

ix   Cameron, K. (2012) Positive Leadership. San Francisco, CA: Berrett-Koehler.

x   Quinn, R. (2015). The Positive Organization. San Francisco, CA: Berrett-Koehler.

xi   Dutton, J. Heaphy, E (2003). The power of high quality connections. In K. Cameron, J. Dutton, & R.Quinn (Eds). Positive organizational scholarship (pp.263-278). San Francisco, CA: Berrett-Koehler.

xii   Gittell, J.F. (2003). The Southwest Airlines way: Using the power of relationships to achieve high performance. New York:McGraw-Hill. Kahn, W.A. (1990). Psychological conditions of personal engagement and disengagement at work. Academy of Management Journal, 33, 692-724.

xiii   Lablanca, G., Umphress, E. & Kaufmann, J. (2000). A preliminary test of the negative asymmetry hypothesis in workplace social networks. Paper presented at the National Academy of Management, Toronto.

xiv   Putnam, R.D. (2000). Bowling alone: The collapse and revival of American community. New York: Simon & Schuster.

xv   Baker, W. E., & Bulkley, N. (2014). Paying it forward vs. rewarding reputation: mechanisms of generalized reciprocity. Organization Science,25(5), 1493-1510.   Contact Humax Corporate to learn more about the use of the Reciprocity Ring™ in organizational settings. https://www.humaxnetworks.com

xvi   Personal communications with authors (2015)

xvii   Rogers, E. (2003). Diffusion of Innovations, Fifth Edition. New York: Free Press.

xviii Gladwell, M. (2000). The Tipping Point: How Little Things Can Make a Big Difference. New York: Little, Brown and Company

Dr. Amy Young

Dr. Amy Young is a faculty member at the Stephen M. Ross School of Business, at the University of Michigan where she incorporates positive psychology, business, and technology in courses. She is a faculty affiliate at University of Michigan's Center for Positive Organizations. Professor Young teaches communication to BBA and MBA students in the areas of digital communication systems, organizational communication, and organizational agility.

Dr. Young's research focuses on organizational communication, digital technology, and positive organizational practices. Dr. Young serves as an Executive Research Advisor to International Data Corporation, an advisory firm specializing in business information technology and communication. She has consulted with numerous Fortune 500 companies including Kellogg, Honeywell, Abbott Pharmaceuticals, UTC, AMEX, Unilever, PwC, Sigel & Gale, and many others.

Dr. Mary Hinesly

Dr. Hinesly has been with the Ross School of Business at the University of Michigan for over a dozen years. She teaches digital business systems, processes and communication.

She has over 20 years in the private sector and was a COO in the retail industry. Dr. Hinesly has served as the Director of Research for Thompson Associates, and the Director of Educational Content and Research for the National Retail Federation.

Dr. Hinesly is a highly requested consultant, presenter and coach on the topic of business, leadership, innovation, communication and technology. She has been involved with over 100 companies with digital transformation including Google, Cisco, Amazon, Jive, Microsoft, Kellogg's, PwC, Wacker, GE, Unilever, LVMH, The New York Times, and more. She presents workshops and seminars for executives. Her research and consulting work focus on business communication and digital transformation.

Michael J. O'Brien

Michael J. O'Brien is the president and founder of Star Performance Group, an international organizational capital consulting firm. Star Performance specializes in leadership, culture and alignment.

He was appointed the Director of Research for The Pacific Institute, a leading organization specializing in the use of positive psychology and neuroscience to help people, teams and organizations develop their mindset and achieve extraordinary results.

With over 32 years of consulting work, O'Brien has grown into a sought after global leadership and culture expert, enabling hundreds of organizations to achieve their goals through transforming their culture. He has conducted face-to-face coaching with over 3,000 senior executives on six continents helping them improve their leadership and ability to drive culture transformations.

He completed his Masters of Education at The University of Western Ontario in Canada and his undergraduate work in finance and economics where he was also an Academic Senator at the School of Business and Economics, Wilfird Laurier University in Canada.

CPSIA information can be obtained at www.ICGtesting.com
Printed in the USA
BVOW05s2058061016

464363BV00003B/27/P